SCIENCE FILES

energy

WATER POWER

Please visit our web site at: www.garethstevens.com
For a free color catalog describing Gareth Stevens Publishing's
list of high-quality books and multimedia programs,
call 1-800-542-2595 (USA) or 1-800-387-3178 (Canada).
Gareth Stevens Publishing's fax: (414) 332-3567.

Library of Congress Cataloging-in-Publication Data

Parker, Steve.
    Water power / by Steve Parker.
        p. cm. — (Science files. Energy)
    Includes bibliographical references and index.
    ISBN 0-8368-4033-X (lib. bdg.)
    Summary: Discusses traditional and developing ways of using water power and ways to preserve this
precious resource.
    1. Water-power—Juvenile literature. 2. Water-supply—Juvenile literature. [1. Water power.
2. Water supply.] I. Title.
    TC147.P37   2004
    621.2'0422—dc22

                                                                    2003060561

This North American edition first published in 2004 by
Gareth Stevens Publishing
A World Almanac Education Group Company
330 West Olive Street, Suite 100
Milwaukee, WI 53212 USA

Original edition © 2002 by David West Children's Books. First published in Great Britain
in 2002 by Heinemann Library, Halley Court, Jordan Hill, Oxford OX2 8EJ, a division
of Reed Educational and Professional Publishing Limited. This U.S. edition © 2004 by
Gareth Stevens, Inc. Additional end matter © 2004 by Gareth Stevens, Inc.

David West Editor: James Pickering
Picture Research: Carrie Haines, Carlotta Cooper
Gareth Stevens Editor: Carol Ryback
Gareth Stevens Designer: Kami Koenig
Cover Design: Melissa Valuch

Photo Credits:
Abbreviations: (t) top, (m) middle, (b) bottom, (l) left, (r) right

CORBIS: Front cover, 3, 4(t), 5(tr), 5(b), 6(bl), 6(ml), 6(mr), 6(br), 7(tl), 7(tr), 7(bl), 8(tr), 9(tl), 9(m),
10–11(t), 12(bl), 13(tl), 13(br), 15(ml), 15(br), 16(bl), 17(tl), 17(br), 20(tr), 22(br), 26(br).
Popperfoto/Reuters: 4(b), 18–19(t).
Cavendish Laboratory, University of Cambridge: 6(b).
Sally Morgan/Ecoscene: 9(br).
Robert Harding Picture Library: 10–11(b), 12–13(b), 14(tr), 18(mr), 21(br), 29(tr); Michael Jenner 11(tr);
Walter Rawlings 11(ml), 23(tr); Pierre Tetrel 11(br); M. H. Black 13(mr); G. Corrigan 19(br), 20–21;
Simon Harris 21(tr); I. Griffiths 22(tl); Paolo Koch 22(tr); Robert Francis 22–23; Louis Salou 28–29.
M. Watson/Ardea London Ltd: 15(tr), 20b(l).

Printed in the United States of America

1 2 3 4 5 6 7 8 9 08 07 06 05 04

SCIENCE FILES

energy

WATER POWER

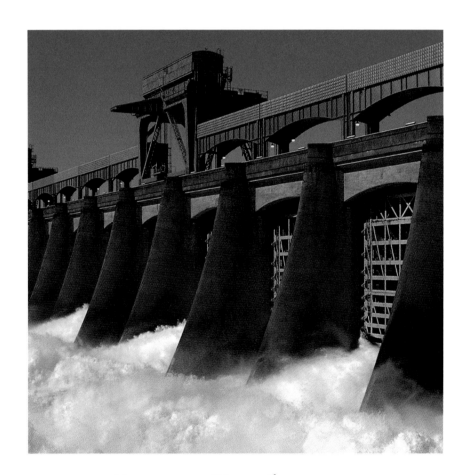

Steve Parker

Gareth Stevens Publishing
A WORLD ALMANAC EDUCATION GROUP COMPANY

CONTENTS

WHAT IS WATER? 6

THE WATER CYCLE 8

MOVING WATER 10

STOPPING WATER 12

HYDROELECTRIC DAM 14

WATER TO ELECTRICITY 16

WORLD WATER USE 18

WATER NEEDS ENERGY! 20

WATER AND STEAM 22

WATER ENGINES 24

WAVE POWER 26

TIDAL POWER 28

FUTURE WATER ENERGY 30

GLOSSARY 31

BOOKS AND WEB SITES 31

INDEX 32

The pent-up power of water behind a dam is released as needed. Trapped water is also useful for drinking, farming, and recreation.

Channels, dams, and locks control water flow. Water management is a costly, ongoing process that uses a lot of energy and many resources.

INTRODUCTION

Water is everywhere — in streams, rivers, lakes, and oceans. It's in our air and sky as clouds, fog, rain, or snow. We drink it, eat it, wash with it. Our bodies are two-thirds water. This amazing substance is not only vital for all forms of life, but also vital as a source of energy. We harness moving water to run machinery and generate electricity. In the future, splitting apart water may give us a new form of energy.

In a hydroelectric power plant, water rushes through rows of giant turbines, which spin the generators to make electricity.

Crashing waves carry massive amounts of energy that can pound cliffs and smash solid rock.

WHAT IS WATER?

Pure water has no smell, no taste, and no color. It's usually a liquid that changes shape and flows — but water is not always liquid.

WATER TAKES DIFFERENT FORMS

Water is a unique substance because it naturally exists in three states, depending on temperature: liquid, solid, or gas. Very cold water can freeze and turn into a hard solid — ice. Very hot water can boil and turn into a vapor, or gas — steam. We are most familiar with liquid water, which is also an amazing solvent. This means that other substances, such as salt or sugar dissolve — or "melt" — into water and seem to disappear.

Long ago, people thought that everything in the world was made of four single, pure substances — earth, air, fire, and water. These were known as the "four elements." In 1784, scientist Henry Cavendish showed that water contained two even simpler substances: hydrogen and oxygen.

H_2O

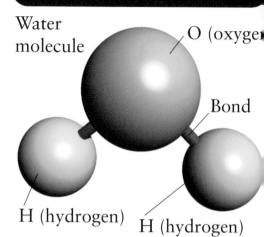

Water molecule

O (oxygen)

Bond

H (hydrogen)   H (hydrogen)

A water molecule (the smallest amount of water that still behaves like water) consists of two hydrogen atoms (H_2) and one oxygen atom (O) bonded together. One drop of water contains billions of molecules of water.

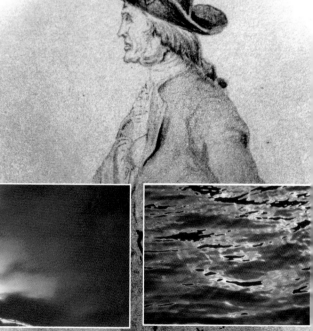

Henry Cavendish, 1731–1810

EARTH

AIR

FIRE   *WATER*

Water boils at 100° C (212° F).

100
90
80
70
60
50
40

Steam from a hot spring is a mix of tiny water droplets and boiling-hot water vapor.

Icicles, snow, hail, and frost are all forms of solid water that occur in nature.

Green **ISSUES**

Pollutants and waste gases that we pump into the environment are causing our entire world to slowly heat up. Global warming may melt the giant ice sheets at the North and South Poles. As sea levels rise, the extra water could cover low islands and flood coasts.

Ice sheets melting in Antarctica

THE CELSIUS SCALE

Water's changing state, or form, is so much a part of our lives that it is the basis for the way we measure temperatures. Water's freezing point — when it changes into ice — is zero (0°) on a Celsius thermometer (32° F). Water's boiling point — when it changes into steam — is 100° on a Celsius thermometer (212° F).

30
20
10
0

Water freezes at 0° C (32° F).

GO WITH THE FLOW

Liquid water flows very easily and always takes the shape of its container. Water also spreads out over a flat surface — as we know when we spill a drink. Liquid water's ability to flow is very important. It means water moves — and anything that moves has energy.

THE WATER CYCLE

Water is always coming and going. Rain falls and soaks into the ground. Ponds fill in winter and dry up in summer. Puddles vanish in hot sunshine. Water flows out of the faucet and down the drain.

NO "NEW" WATER

The water we use for drinking, cooking, and washing is the same water that dinosaurs drank or swam in. "Old" water is never destroyed, and "new" water is never made. It only changes form — liquid, solid, or vapor — as it moves around the world and through our atmosphere. This constant water movement is called the water cycle.

Water flows fastest and has the most energy when it falls straight down, as in a waterfall.

The Sun powers the water cycle. Solar heat evaporates liquid water. As the water vapor rises, it cools and condenses, or changes, back into a liquid.

Rivers are grooves that carry rain and groundwater down to lakes and oceans.

Water over water — tiny floating drops form clouds above the ocean.

Ocean water evaporates. Rivers flow to oceans.

Plant life produces water vapor.

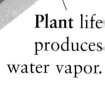

Water freezes on cold mountaintops.

SOLAR POWER

Water is constantly "drying up" — changing from liquid to vapor and floating up into the air. Even in very cold climates, solar heat is always at work, melting ice and snow into liquid, and causing evaporation. The Sun's warmth gives water energy and makes it move.

Rain falls when the drops in a cloud become too heavy to float.

Groundwater is water that soaks into soil and rocks. It flows slowly downhill like an underground river.

Lake water looks still, but it is slowly moving.

Lakes provide water with a large surface area for evaporation.

Green ISSUES

Deforestation — clear cutting huge areas of trees and other growth — is occurring at terrifying rates, especially in tropical rain forests. Without tree roots to hold the soil and soak up rainwater, soil washes into rivers, clogging them. Plants die. The area is destroyed for many years.

Deforestation destruction

UP, DOWN, AND ALL ALONG

Solar heat slowly changes liquid water in rivers, lakes, and oceans into water vapor. The vapor rises and blows in the wind. Colder air higher up makes the vapor condense into tiny drops of liquid that float as clouds. As the drops clump together, they get heavier and fall as rain or snow to rivers, lakes, and oceans. The cycle repeats.

MOVING WATER

Dip your hand in a stream to feel the power of running water. For more than two thousand years, people have harnessed this energy by using waterwheels.

ANCIENT IDEA

The first waterwheels turned in the Middle East, ancient Rome, and China. Their use spread across Europe and Asia. By the year A.D. 1087, about five thousand waterwheels powered machines and mills in England.

Too much energy: Niagara Falls would smash any waterwheel to pieces.

WATERWHEEL DESIGNS

Undershot waterwheel

The waterwheel is usually two wheels with paddles or blades around the rim. In the undershot design, the water goes past the base of the wheel. In the overshot version, water pours over the top. The overshot design requires a greater drop in water height.

Direction of water flow

Turning wheel provides power for machinery.

A strong current, or race, powers this waterwheel.

WATERWHEEL LIMITS

Nature provides us with plenty of "free"

energy in the form of moving water. The Industrial Revolution started in the 1700s by using water to power machines. Water power has practical limits. The flow must be reliable all year. A flood will smash a waterwheel, while a drought leaves it idle. Machines, such as millstones that grind wheat, or weaving looms that make cloth, had to be located next to flowing water. Factories that ran on water power were often built in hilly, wet landscapes.

Ancient TECHNOLOGY

Waterwheels were made of wood, so few ancient ones survive. Their water flow often came from specially built channels or pipes, bringing the energy to where it was needed.

Giant waterwheel, Syria

RAISING WATER

The waterlift is as old as the waterwheel. A source of energy moves or raises the water by turning a waterwheel or device called an Archimedes screw (basically, a curved ramp). Both are useful for providing drinking water or water for crops.

In the waterlift, energy from animals or machines turns a wheel (above) or a screw (right). This raises water from a well or channel. ▶

Direction of rotation

Handle turned

Water is drawn up

STOPPING WATER

Running water carries a lot of force and is difficult to stop. River dams hold back the flow with thick, strong walls. The pent-up water is, in effect, stored energy.

WHY BUILD DAMS?

Modern dams have many uses. Dams produce energy, help control flooding, and lessen the effects of droughts. Humans, food crops, and farm animals all need and use the large amounts of water backed up by a dam. Giant dams are some of the biggest structures ever built — and the water backed up by them can provide hours of great fun!

Workers build an embankment dam (see below) in Swaziland, Africa.

INSIDE A DAM

The embankment dam is a simple type of gravity dam. It relies on its great weight, rather than a specialized shape, to hold back the water. Its construction can be adapted to local building materials and it needs little special machinery. The waterproof, clay core prevents slow seepage.

Lake Nasser behind the Aswan High Dam on the Nile is more than 300 miles (500 km) long.

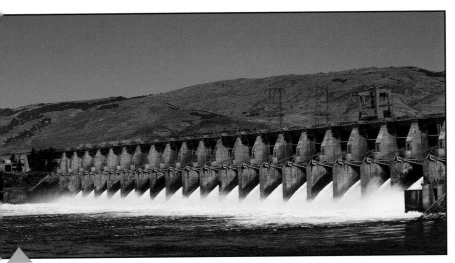

Buttresses (the fin-like structures) give strength to the main, thin wall of this dam in Oregon.

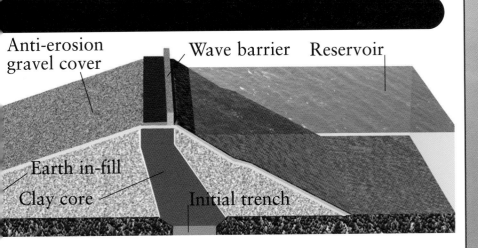

Anti-erosion gravel cover

Wave barrier   Reservoir

Earth in-fill

Clay core   Initial trench

WHERE ARE DAMS BUILT?

A dam is usually built across a river's narrowest section in an area that has high banks, such as in a canyon or a gorge. This uses fewer materials. Low areas behind the dam fill to form a lake, or reservoir. Planners must take care that the dam does not flood entire cities.

Tarbela Dam, on the mighty Indus River in northern Pakistan, is the largest dam built in the earth-filled embankment design.

Green ISSUES

The reservoir, or lake, behind a dam floods a huge area that may contain ancient monuments, special wildlife, and other precious sites. In rare cases, entire villages and endangered animals are moved to escape the rise of the water.

A drought caused low water levels in this reservoir.

The double-curve shape of Hoover Dam on the Colorado River resists water pressure.

HYDROELECTRIC DAM

A hydroelectric power plant uses water ("hydro") to spin the turbines that generate electricity. While waterwheels were built right next to the moving water, a hydroelectric plant transmits (sends) its power great distances along a grid of wires.

Spillways allow extra water to get through the dam in times of flooding or high water levels.

THE HYDROELECTRIC DAM AND POWER PLANT

Water held back by the dam forms a reservoir. The deeper the reservoir, the greater the water pressure at its base. This water blasts along tunnels under the main dam to spin turbines in the power plant (see page 16). The reservoir provides a "reserve" of water so that the power plant keeps generating power, even in times of drought.

Sluice gates control flow of water into tunnels.

Secondary barrage for maintenance and flood control

Tunnels under main dam channel water to turbines.

Main clay-core earth-embankment dam

Reservoir

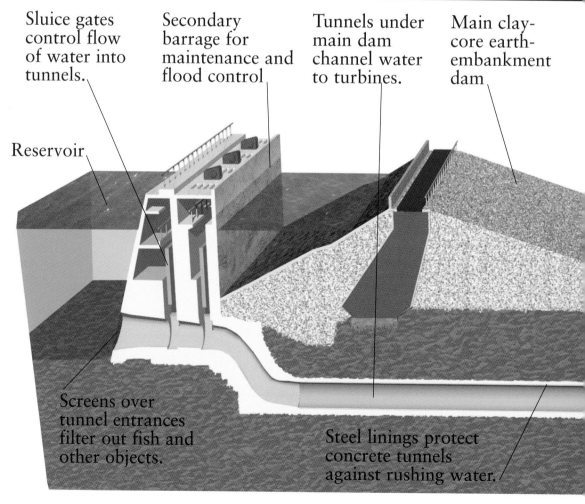

Screens over tunnel entrances filter out fish and other objects.

Steel linings protect concrete tunnels against rushing water.

14

CHANGE OF ENERGY

Hydroelectricity uses the energy of moving water — which comes from the Sun's warmth — to generate power. Turbines harness the water's motion and generators change that movement into electrical energy (see next page). From Norway to New Zealand, places with many fast-flowing rivers produce more than nine-tenths of their electricity using hydroelectric power plants.

(see next page)

Control room staff monitor the turbines and generators, matching electrical output with demand.

Green ISSUES

Many fish and other animals migrate, or travel, along rivers to breed. Dams block their way. A row of small waterfalls and channels, or "fish ladders," helps them return to spawn.

Salmon leap natural falls.

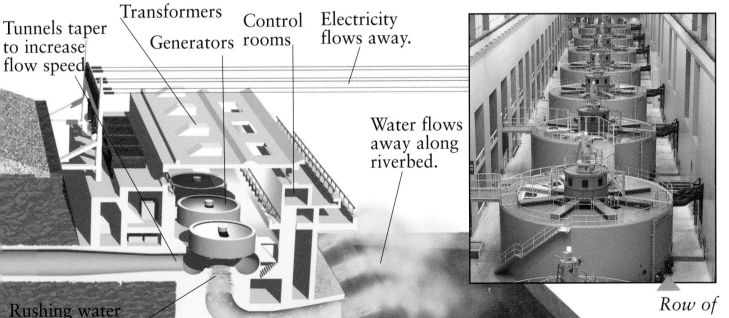

Tunnels taper to increase flow speed.

Transformers

Generators

Control rooms

Electricity flows away.

Water flows away along riverbed.

Rushing water spins turbines.

Row of generator-turbines

15

WATER TO ELECTRICITY

Hydroelectricity is not made from water itself. It comes from the energy of moving water. After water gives up some of its energy, it flows on to the ocean to continue its part in the water cycle. Hydroelectricity is a long-term, sustainable form of energy.

TURBINES

The key parts of the hydroelectric power plant are the dam (see previous page), turbines, and generators. Turbines function much like huge fans with angled blades. Each turbine in a hydroelectric plant has a central shaft that spins as water flows past.

Power lines supported by towers carry away electricity from the Dallas Dam hydroelectric power plant.

(see previous page)

Green ISSUES

A hydroelectric power plant is one of the cleanest ways to produce electricity. It does not burn fossil fuels that create air pollution and greenhouse gases. One drawback is the effect of the dam. It can flood upstream areas, reduce downstream water flow, and interfere with wildlife migration patterns.

TURBINE TYPES

Turbines are designed with various shapes and layouts of blades, shaft, and casings to obtain the most energy from different speeds and pressures of flowing water. The impulse wheel version is similar to the traditional waterwheel.

Kaplan axial-flow turbine (upright shaft)

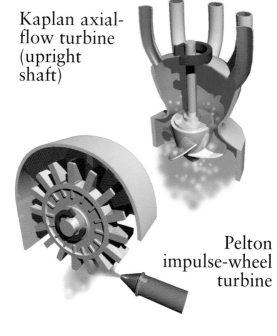

Pelton impulse-wheel turbine

GENERATORS

Water power pushes the turbine blades and spins them on their shaft, just like moving air — wind — turns a windmill. The turbine's shaft is connected to the generator, which changes the kinetic (moving) energy of the rotating shaft into electrical energy. Usually one turbine spins one generator on the same shaft. Some power plants have several turbines linked by gears to one generator.

Fossil fuels cause air pollution.

THE GENERATOR

Magnetism and electricity are different parts of the force called electromagnetism. Moving magnets cause electricity to flow through wire, and flowing electricity magnetizes a wire. Generators produce electricity by electromagnetic induction — a spinning rotor moves electromagnets past a set of wires. The stator creates even more electricity in its stationary wire coils.

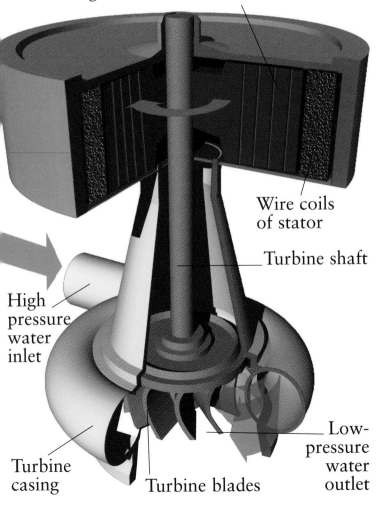

Electromagnet wire coils of rotor

Wire coils of stator

Turbine shaft

High pressure water inlet

Low-pressure water outlet

Turbine casing

Turbine blades

Transformers alter the electricity produced by the generators by increasing the force, or voltage, that travels along power lines.

WORLD WATER USE

Water is so important to life that it is rarely used as simply an energy source. Hydroelectric systems, with their power plants and dams, often play a part in making water available for other uses.

ON THE FARM

One of water's most valuable uses is for irrigation to grow farm crops, such as rice or soybeans. Water stored in the reservoir during the wet season is gradually released into nearby fields during the dry season. Farm animals also require large amounts of water on a daily basis.

West India's Narmada River project includes one of the world's largest concrete dams. The dam holds back water during the monsoon (windy and rainy season) and helps prevent flooding.

PUMPED STORAGE

Pumped storage uses pumps to move the stored water supply around to meet demand for electricity. When demand is high, water flows down from the upper reservoir to generate electricity. During times of low demand, pumps use "spare" electricity from the network to pump the water back to the upper storage reservoir.

Surge tunnel

Lower reservoir

Upper reservoir

Upper pumping station

Turbines

Lower pumping station

The Three Gorges Dam over China's Yangtze River in China is 600 feet (183 meters) high and 1.5 miles (2.3 kilometers) long. It will have twenty-six giant turbines.

Farmland in Argentina suffered a common problem – sudden heavy rain, then a long drought. The Cerros Colorados Dam stores the water to produce a more even, year-round flow. Its power plant supplies the city of Buenos Aires, which is 621 miles (1,000 km) away.

IN THE CITY

Water fills many needs: drinking, cooking, washing, cleaning, and sanitary needs. Every day, each person in a developed country uses at least 25 gallons (100 liters) of water. Huge cities need enormous supplies, which come from dam reservoirs.

Green ISSUES

All plants need water, and the world's main food crops need more than most. When rains fail, water from a reservoir flows through sluice gates into fields to soak the soil. Using stored water causes fewer problems than pumping out groundwater.

Lush greenery all year

WATER NEEDS ENERGY!

Water is a source of energy — but it also uses energy. It takes an enormous amount of energy to collect, filter, purify, and pump water to our homes, businesses, and industries. All these processes not only use electricity and other forms of energy, but also chemicals, machinery, and raw materials. Water is big business!

JOBS IN WATER

Millions of people work in the water business. In addition to dams and power plants, other water-based industries include water treatment plants, pumping stations, and storage towers. Also, millions of miles (kilometers) of buried pipes and sewers need regular maintenance.

Industries such as papermaking (top) and farming (above) use far more water than ordinary homes, offices, and schools. In factories, water is used to clean, dissolve, lubricate (like oil), and as a coolant to carry away heat.

Wastewater must be treated to remove germs and poisons. Solid leftovers can be dried and spread on the land as fertilizer.

Ancient TECHNOLOGY

Two thousand years ago, ancient Romans understood the need for water that did not carry germs or spread diseases. The Romans built long channels that brought clean water from remote areas into their cities. They bridged valleys with high structures called aqueducts.

Pont du Gard aqueduct, southern France

FRESH WATER FROM SALTY

Water covers 70 percent of Earth's surface, but because most of it is salty, we cannot directly use it. The process of removing the salt from ocean water is called desalination (de-salting). A desalination plant consumes (uses) a lot of energy as it produces pure water.

DESALINATION (DE-SALTING)

"Reverse osmosis" (see diagram) is one desalination method. Ocean water is pumped into a tank with a membrane that holds back the salts and minerals but permits liquids and water to flow through. This liquid is heated to a vapor and condensed to pure, fresh water.

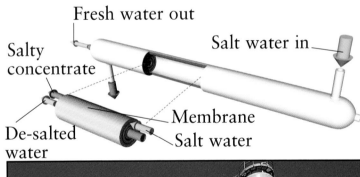

Fresh water out

Salt water in

Salty concentrate

De-salted water

Membrane
Salt water

Desalination towers cool vapor into water.

WATER AND STEAM

When energy is added to water, it produces a powerful force that can drive machines, engines, and vehicles. This added energy is heat — and the force is steam.

Wairakei geothermal power plant, one of the world's largest, supplies one-twentieth of New Zealand's electricity.

In the late 1800s, steam-powered farm machinery replaced horses — then diesel replaced steam.

START THE REVOLUTION

Steam was a vital power source during the Industrial Revolution of the 1700s. Steam engines powered newly invented machines as factories, industries, and mass production spread around the world. In the 1800s, the same thing happened to transportation systems when steam power on wheels — railroads — spread across the continents. Steam engines produce a lot of waste energy in the form of heat. Natural steam is still used to generate electricity in some areas.

A geyser's hot water and spurting steam boils up from deep underground.

Green **ISSUES**

Places with natural hot springs, geysers, or red-hot rocks near the surface have a free supply of geothermal or "ground-heat" energy. This heat is used directly in the area to warm homes, schools, and public places. It can also be converted to electricity and transported long distances.

Geothermal trap, France

GEOTHERMAL POWER

Cool water is pumped down into cracks in the rocks (1). Rocks deep underground are much hotter than those at the surface (2). Great pressures at depth also heat the water, changing it to a gas (3). Pipes gather rising steam and vapors for use in generating electricity at the power plant (4).

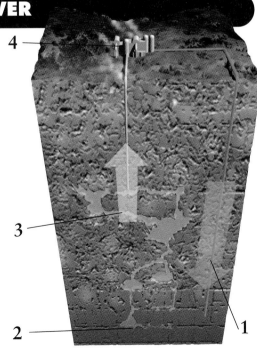

EARTH'S HEAT

Deep in Earth, rocks are very hot — as we see when a volcano erupts. A geothermal power plant traps super-hot water or steam rising from these layers to spin turbines. We can only harness the energy of a few of the geothermal areas around the globe.

WATER ENGINES

Most car engines run on fossil fuel (gasoline or diesel), waste heat energy, and emit (give off) many harmful exhaust fumes. In the future, hydrogen fuel cells may power our vehicles. The hydrogen comes from water. Hydrogen fuel cells produce electricity that powers a quiet, efficient motor. Best of all, the exhaust from these engines is water.

Green **ISSUES**

Exhaust fumes from gasoline and diesel engines contain carbon dioxide and other "greenhouse gases." Engine fumes also contain carbon monoxide — a poisonous gas — and many chemicals that not only increase pollution, but also cause acid rain and smog.

Several car makers are testing "no emission" (NE) vehicles that do not emit dangerous fumes and vapors. Hazardous chemicals spewed out from cars, trucks, and buses build up in heavy traffic areas and may cause health problems.

Increased use of NE vehicles are especially important in big cities with daily traffic jams. Gasoline and diesel engines emit harmful exhaust continuously — even when traffic is stopped at lights.

Los Angeles smog

NE cars test fuel-cell engines.

RUNNING ON WATER

A fuel cell has few moving parts. It works by adding hydrogen gas fuel to the oxygen gas in air. Fuel cells produce water — released as a vapor — plus energy in the form of electricity that drives the motor.

Fuel cell problems include how to produce, transport, and store the hydrogen. Electricity is used to split water into hydrogen and oxygen gases. Transporting hydrogen gas can be a safety hazard. Finally, hydrogen gas requires huge amounts of storage space on vehicles.

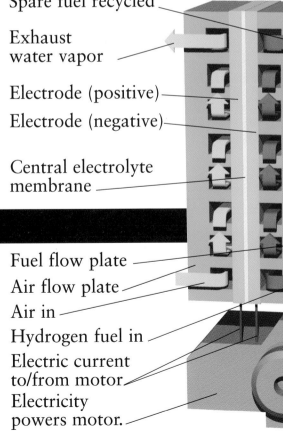

Spare fuel recycled

Exhaust
water vapor

Electrode (positive)

Electrode (negative)

Central electrolyte
membrane

Fuel flow plate

Air flow plate

Air in

Hydrogen fuel in

Electric current
to/from motor

Electricity
powers motor.

Quiet, clean, efficient — a fuel-cell car

HOW FUEL CELLS WORK

A fuel cell works like a hydrogen-powered battery. Hydrogen fuel flows though one side, and air containing oxygen flows through the other. A central sheet, the electrolyte membrane, allows the two gases to combine and release tiny bits of atoms called electrons. These move only one way, so the process sets up a regular flow of electrons — which is an electric current.

WAVE POWER

Any form of moving water has energy. Waves are caused by winds blowing over the ocean's surface. Solar energy causes winds. As sunshine heats rising air, cooler air blows along as wind to take its place. In this way, the energy of waves — just like the energy in a flowing river — originally came from the Sun.

DIFFICULT TO HARNESS

A river with a dam provides a continuous, smooth flow of energy to convert into electricity. By contrast, wave energy is extreme and unpredictable. Gales of wind and giant breakers may follow calm days. Wave power is sustainable and pollution free, and it has little effect on the environment, but harnessing the varied and violent wave power poses great challenges.

Problems, PROBLEMS

Storms create massive waves — some taller than houses — that crash down with rock-shattering force. Waves have damaged several "test" wave generators, and saltwater quickly eats away (corrodes) many metals.

A big wave contains hundreds of tons of water.

SHORELINE DESIGN

Pressure differences in the air trapped by the alternating rise and fall of a wave's water level drives a shoreline generator. Wave height changes cause a "blow and suck" movement of air that powers a turbine. The turbine's shaft spins the generator. This shoreline design is useful on remote islands, but daily tides limit its reliability.

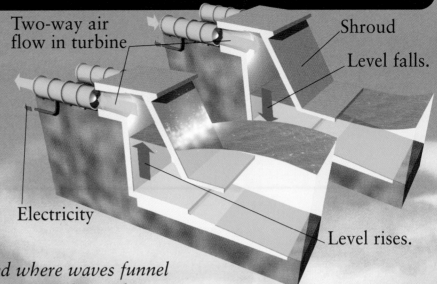

Two-way air flow in turbine

Shroud

Level falls.

Electricity

Level rises.

A shoreline generator must be located where waves funnel into a channel in the rocks. An inset picture shows the rear view.

TIDAL POWER

Another way to harness the energy of moving water for electricity is through the use of tidal power. These tidal forces provide a more reliable and steady source of power than wave energy (see previous page).

WHERE OCEANS MEET RIVERS

As the sea level rises with an incoming tide, saltwater meets freshwater at the mouth, or estuary, of a river. During low tide, the water level falls and the river water resumes its journey to the ocean. Water flow caused by these changing levels acts like a two-way river that can generate electricity. Risks include storm damage and environmental effects.

WHY TIDES HAPPEN

The forces of gravity from the Moon and Sun create tides. The Moon's gravity pulls on Earth's water and causes a bulge. When the Sun and the Moon are at a right angle (90°) to each other, their gravities act against each other and produce a "neap" tide with a small range. When the Moon and Sun line up, their combined gravitational forces cause an extra-high and extra-low "spring" tide.

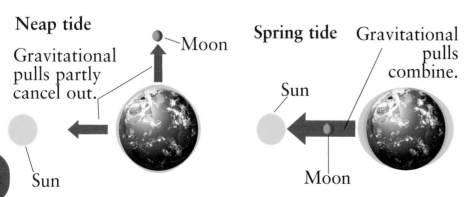

Neap tide

Gravitational pulls partly cancel out.

Moon

Sun

Spring tide

Gravitational pulls combine.

Sun

Moon

THE TIDAL BARRAGE

Much like a hydroelectric dam on a river, a tidal barrage also powers turbines and generators. As the tide falls, the strength and height of water flowing from a river to the ocean increases to a peak over three hours, then slows over the next three hours. As the tide rises, the process repeats — but in the other direction. A barrage can also links two banks of an estuary. A gap in the barrage allows boats to pass.

The LaRance Tidal Power Station in Saint Malo, France, is a tidal barrage that has been producing electricity since 1966.

Green ISSUES

A tidal barrage smooths out water level changes along the banks of a river and the nearby coast. This affects shore animals such as fish, crabs, shellfish, and wading birds that probe the mud for worms and other food.

Crabs greet a rising tide.

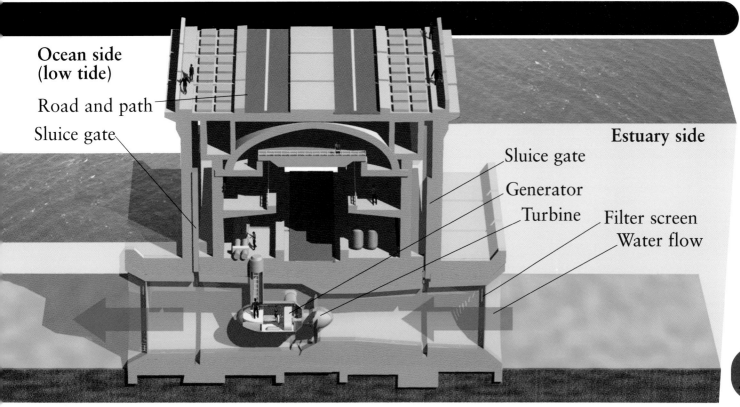

Ocean side (low tide)

Road and path

Sluice gate

Estuary side

Sluice gate

Generator

Turbine

Filter screen

Water flow

29

FUTURE WATER ENERGY

Can water provide energy for our future needs as coal, oil, and other fossil-fuel reserves run out? There are only so many rivers to dam for hydroelectricity — so we must explore other methods.

ULTIMATE ENERGY?

Solar heat creates global winds and powers massive water currents, called gyres. The process of efficiently trapping the ocean's enormous energy is an ongoing, gigantic task for engineers. Their successful efforts could result in huge amounts of clean, "green" electricity far into the future.

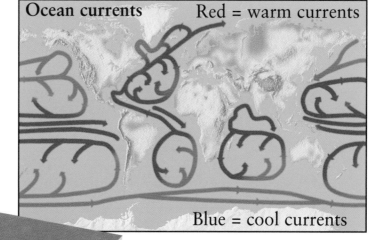

Ocean currents   Red = warm currents

Blue = cool currents

Underwater turbine

Current

Anchor cables

Electricity

THERMAL GIANT

Deep ocean water is much colder than surface waters. This huge temperature difference may someday spin turbines in an offshore heat exchanger. Gas bubbles blown down would force deep water to the surface.

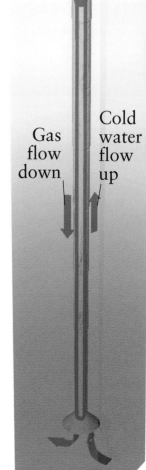

Warm surface water

Turbines and generators

Heat exchanger

Cold seabed water

Gas flow down

Cold water flow up

CURRENT TURBINES

Underwater turbines similar to those in hydroelectric power plants might work in regions with powerful, steady ocean currents. Problems to overcome include the tremendous forces of water pressure and the corrosive effect of saltwater on metal.

GLOSSARY

stuary: the "mouth" of a river; where the river flows into the ocean.

vaporate: to change from a liquid state into a gas or vapor.

lobal warming: the rise in average daily temperature around the world thought to be caused by pollution.

reenhouse gases: chemicals in the atmosphere (air) that trap the Sun's heat rather than letting it escape into space.

duction: creating electricity by the action of a spinning object within a magnetic field.

molecule: the smallest amount that displays all the properties of that substance.

purification: the act of making a substance pure by removing all other substances.

reverse osmosis: the separation of fluids using a special membrane that permits the lower-concentrated fluid to govern the process.

solvent: a liquid that dissolves a solid.

sustainable: able to continue for a very long time without running out or wearing away.

turbine: a type of heavy machinery with fan-like, angled blades attached to a central shaft that spins when under pressure from air, wind, or liquids.

vapor: a gas that can contain chemicals and that can change into a liquid by cooling.

MORE BOOKS TO READ

The Hoover Dam. Great Building Feats (series). Lesley A. Dutemple (Lerner)

Hydropower of the Future: New Ways of Turning Water into Energy. Allison Stark Draper (Rosen)

The Water Cycle. Trudi Strain Trueit (Franklin Watts)

Water Power. Energy Forever (series). Ian S. Graham (Raintree/Steck Vaughn)

WEB SITES

Discover more about hydropower and visit a series of links regarding renewable energy. *www.eid.doe.gov/kids/renewabl/renewable _links.html#Hydroelectric*

Check out the Hydropower/Water Energy Projects for a variety of science activities. *www.energyquest.ca.gov/projects#hydro*

Due to the dynamic nature of the Internet, some web sites stay current longer than others. To find additional web sites, use a reliable search engine with one or more of the following keywords: *Bay of Fundy, Hoover Dam, hydroelectric power, renewable energy, Three Gorges Dam, waves.*

INDEX

acid rain 24
aqueducts 21
Archimedes screw 11
Argentina 19
Aswan High Dam 12

boiling 6, 7
Buenos Aires, Argentina 19
buttresses 13

Cavendish, Henry 6
Cerros Colorados Dam 19
clouds 5, 8, 9
condensation 8, 21

dams 4, 12–13, 14, 15, 16,
     18–19, 20, 26, 28, 29, 30
deforestation 9
desalination 21
dissolving 6, 20

electricity 5, 16, 17, 18, 20,
     22, 23, 28, 30
     fuel cell 24–25
     hydroelectric power
          5, 14, 15, 16, 18
     tidal power 28
evaporation 8, 21

factories 20, 22
faucets 8
fossil fuels 16, 30
freezing 6, 7, 9
freshwater 21
fuel cells 24, 25

generators 15, 17, 27, 29
geothermal power 22–23

geysers 7, 22, 23
global warming 7
gravity 28
greenhouse gases 16, 24
groundwater 9

hail 7
heat-exchanger 30
Hoover Dam 13
hydroelectricity 5, 14, 15,
     16, 18, 30
hydrogen 6, 24, 25

ice 6, 7
Industrial Revolution 11, 22
industries 20, 22
irrigation 18

Lake Nasser 12
lakes 5, 8, 9, 12, 13

Middle East 10
monsoons 18

Narmada River, India 18
NE ("No Emission")
     vehicles 24
Nile River 12
North Pole 7

ocean currents 30
oceans 5, 8, 9, 16, 21, 26
oxygen 6, 25

Pakistan 13
pollution 7, 16, 24
purification 20

rain 5, 8, 9, 18, 19
reservoirs 13, 14, 18, 19
rivers 5, 8, 9, 12, 13, 15,
     26, 28, 29, 30

saltwater 21, 26, 30
sea levels 7, 27, 28, 29
shoreline design 27
snow 5, 7
solar 8, 9, 26, 30
solvent 6
South Pole 7
springs 7
steam 6, 7, 22, 23
steam engines 22
Sun 8, 9, 15, 26,
     28, 30
Swaziland, Africa 12
Syria 11

Tarbela Dam 13
temperatures 7
Three Gorges Dam 19
tidal power 17, 28–29
turbines 5, 14, 15, 16, 18,
     19, 23, 28, 29, 30

wastewater treatment 20
water cycle 8–9, 16
waterfalls 8
waterlift 11
water vapor 6, 7, 8, 9,
     21, 25
waterwheels 10, 11
wave power 5, 26–27

Yangtze River, China 19